# LOOKING FOR LOVE IN ALL THE RIGHT PLACES:

*TWENTY-ONE LESSONS ABOUT FINDING LOVE WITHIN*

**By Debra Strother-Yarde**

All Rights Reserved. No part of this publication may be reproduced in any form or by any means, including scanning, photocopying, or otherwise without prior written permission of the copyright holder.

Copyright © 2018

ISBN: 13:978-1986073509

ISBN: 10:1986073505

# DEDICATION

God is first and foremost! He gets all the Glory! Special thanks to my family for all their support. To my daughters, Lakeisha and Jessica, my grandkisses, Amor, Malania, Kayla, and Sophia. My role is to make sure you find love in the right places!

# Table of Contents

Introduction ........................................................................... 1

So, What's My Story? ........................................................... 1

Day 1: Created From The Inside ....................................... 12

Day 2: His Plan For Me ...................................................... 18

Day 3: Created In Christ .................................................... 22

Day 4: My Heart Trusts Him ............................................ 26

Day 5: We All Want To Be Happy ................................... 30

Day 6: Are You Loving The One You're With? ........... 34

Day 7: I Am Worth The Wait ........................................... 38

Day 8: Holiness ................................................................... 42

Day 9: Living A Life Of Freedom .................................... 46

Day 10: His Love Is Unconditional ................................. 50

Day 11: Love Never Fails .................................................. 54

Day 12: My Knight In Shining Armor ........................... 58

Day 13: Devoted Confidence ............................................ 62

Day 14: Moving Forward .................................................. 66

Day 15: Listening In The Right Place ............................. 70

Day 16: Master Yourself .................................................. 74

Day 17: To Love Is To Obey ........................................... 78

Day 18: Making Peace With The Past .......................... 82

Day 19: His Love Is So Amazing ................................... 86

Day 20: I Am Made Whole ............................................ 90

Day 21: No Self-Doubt ................................................... 94

# INTRODUCTION

## SO, WHAT'S MY STORY?

I was born and raised in Madison, Virginia. Growing up in a small town like Madison meant everybody knew everybody. It was a great community with great people.

I am the oldest of four children. For me, being the oldest carries a lot of weight. When we were growing up, I was always looked upon as the one who knew better, so I should have been doing better. My family was very close. Our aunties, uncles, and grandparents all lived in the same rural area. It was a blessing to be close to family. I loved the family gatherings we would have. We had cousins from Washington, DC, that would come and spend time with us every summer. We always had a blast. We were always cutting up. We went to church every Sunday, too, like a typical family. My brothers and sisters and I were very close. We still are today.

I can remember when my brother was born. I felt he started getting more attention than me. When he started crawling and walking, he would break up all my toys. I was really upset with him. I guess, when I was around four and he was around two, I called myself looking after him. While I was watching him, I found an interesting bottle and decided to give him some of the "candy" that was inside. I had no idea that this was actually children's aspirin. Thankfully, my mom came rushing in the room before he had a chance to swallow them. Yes, I had to go in time out for trying to feed my brother aspirin.

Time out for us was our mother sitting us down and talking to us for about thirty minutes, then getting her switches and going to work on our butts. Those were the days when parents could show their authority as parents and not get in trouble. I am so grateful for my parents. I can look back over my childhood and see all they went through and endured just for us. My mom worked three jobs. Dad had his own construction business, so he worked long hours and traveled a lot to different areas as a bricklayer. My childhood is vivid in my mind, as I can remember a lot.

One Christmas, our parents went out of their way to provide us with great memories and unexpected surprises. It was the first time my brother and I were given bikes. We were so excited. My sister wanted a Baby Alive doll. We opened our toys on Christmas morning and were so happy. Unfortunately, that night, we were awakened by the sound of our father's voice saying, "Get up! The house is on fire."

Yes, our home was on fire, and we lost everything, except our bikes. We were so thankful that God had spared our lives. As a family, we endured a lot of hardships, but that kept us together and helped us grow stronger as a family. I am a daddy's girl, so I stayed under him a lot when he was around. My dad taught my brother and I how to work on cars. Yes, I can check oil by myself and change tires by myself. I have two wonderful parents who only want what is best for their children. I think every child should be nurtured and made to feel like they are somebody great and that they can accomplish anything in the world. My parents made me and my siblings feel this way.

For every little girl, the love she receives from her father is so very important. Little girls need that affirmation. I was always told that I was loved. I was always shown that I was loved. But looking back, I can really see where I went wrong in my life and why I was so "messed" up as a young woman. I had everything going for me—a good home, great parents. We went to church every Sunday. But it wasn't about any of that. Even with a firm foundation, things happened. I was a curious child. If my mom told me not to do something, I wanted to know why? I didn't just take her word, so I stayed in timeout. (First, the talk; then, the switches). Yes, I was the rebellious one. That landed me in a lot of heartache and pain. You know, when you rebel against your parents, you are rebelling against God, as well. I can now see the look in my parents' eyes when they had to look for me and could not find me. I say to every young girl who has parents, "Love them. Respect them. Obey them." You were given to your parents for a reason. They might not dot every I and cross every T, but as long as they are providing for you and making sure you have a roof over your head, give them all the love and respect they deserve.

Unfortunately, I was a spoiled brat. I was the first grandchild in the family on both sides, so I got whatever I wanted. I was blessed to be able to know both sets of my grandparents. Yes, it was a blessing. I was adored and loved. So, if I had all of that, what happened to me? Where did I get off track? Why did I get off track? You know we can live in the best of situations and have the best of the best, but as the Word says, "The devil, as a roaring lion, walketh about, seeking whom he may devour" (1 Peter 5:8 King James Bible). Like any teenager, I wanted to do things that I was not mature enough to do. As a result, I experienced things I was too young to handle.

I met this guy and fell madly in love with him. He would call me all the time. Now, my dad was very strict, but we would find a way to talk. I would sneak and talk to him. And when I talked to him, I was on top of the world. I was in love with this guy.

When my birthday was coming up, I asked my mom if I could go out with some friends, just to a hang out. Surprisingly, she agreed, but she said, "Debra, don't play with me. Don't you be out there doing anything that you are not supposed to be doing."

"Ok, Mom. Yes, Mom," was what I said. But you know me, I was going to do what I wanted to do. I might as well be honest. I was the child who gave my parents the worst grief. I hurt them. So, that evening, I went out and disobeyed my mother. When I got home, she looked at me and asked, "Why, Debra?"

I said, "What do you mean, Mom?"

Every mother knows her child. She knew I had gone against her teachings. Most of all, I had disobeyed God. It happened. That one encounter that I had took me off the path of my journey and into a wild spiral of uncertainty. I started looking for love in so many other places. I mean, I could not find any satisfaction. After that one encounter, my life changed. I was lost. I felt rejected and I felt bitter. All the emotions, I felt. After that encounter, I just lost myself. Every other encounter I had was a disappointment, to be honest. I had looked everywhere and could not find it. Notice, I said looked. I was looking for love in all the wrong places, so things in life happened, and then I didn't know the importance of loving me. I didn't love me because I didn't know me. My thought process was so distorted by that one encounter, and no one could reach me. You see, that encounter threw me into a wheel that went around and around, repeating cycle after cycle. So, yes, I was broken and bruised all because of this one encounter. I gave myself to someone for the first time, and I thought that it was love, but I soon found out it was a lie. Then I started looking for a new person to make up for the lie that was told to me by the first person. Again, I fell for another lie. Then, of course, I thought something was wrong with me because of the lie. And I kept looking and looking for the one person to love me, but it never happened. Let me rephrase that—"God has loved us from the beginning. He will never stop loving us. But we must learn to love Him as well."

Ultimately, the bottom line is this—that night, I didn't make the right choice. Those words "I love you" touched a part of my soul. I wanted to be loved and wanted to feel love. When they were conveyed to me, there was an excitement that I felt. Yes, he loves me, I thought. So, because I didn't know the truth, I was easily deceived. The truth was distorted. In my mind, I thought giving of myself to someone was a way to love. Wow! Was I wrong. Let's be honest. I know a lot of young women have experienced this kind of love. They think it is love, but really, it is lust. Let's just be real. I didn't know it was lust because I was young and dumb. All it was, was a moment of pleasure fulfilled. Well, love is not a moment of pleasure.

My problem was I had low self-esteem. I looked for love to fill the emptiness. This happens to so many young women. They try to fill this internal void with alcohol or a variety of drugs. Some will try to fill the void with relationships and sex. Well, I had some problems going on with me. And just could not talk to anyone. I internalized things, and I would not talk about it. I would always think in my mind that no one knew me, that no one understood me, so I used that excuse to block everyone and everything out that was close to me. Yes, I shut down. When I shut down, I stopped caring. That was the worst thing that could have happened to me. I stopped caring about me. And then I didn't care who hurt me. I just let them do whatever they wanted to me because I was looking for love in all the wrong places. Have you ever heard the saying "You have to love yourself before you can love another"? Well, I was loving everybody but me. I withdrew from my family. My academic performance failed. I became bitter, and I felt rejected all because of that one encounter. That one encounter broke me as a young woman. I can remember my mom coming into my room, trying to talk to me, while I lay on my bed, balled up in a little knot. I would not respond to her. I could not because I didn't know how. All I felt was disappointment. I had let her down. But most of all, I had let myself down. You know I have spent a lot of my time trying to make up for that one encounter. I realized that I could not undo what was done because what was done was done. I couldn't change the past.

It is important that every young girl and woman realizes how much God truly loves them. But you must love yourself. If you know your value and your worth, there is nothing or no one that can take you off course. The main point is you must know.

That same night, I was not out by myself. I was with the crew! We all messed up. Trust me, we were all comparing ourselves to each other and trying to outdo one another. How many of you know what that is like? We've all been there.

As I have matured and discovered that I am truly loved and adored by the King of Kings, my life has been restored and renewed. For every woman that will read this book, just know that finding love within is the key to your success and happiness. You can never go wrong when you finally realize how important it is to love you. The fact that God even loves us in spite of all of our flaws is exciting to know. He looks beyond all of that and sees the most beautiful girl in the world. His eye has been on you from day one. This book was written to let you know how important it is to look for love in all the right places. You have to realize that God has had his eye on you since you were in your mother's womb. He has protected you and kept you from danger. Why? Because He loves you. He loves you unconditionally There is nothing He will not do for you. His love is amazing. I fell in love with the Master, and then I fell in love with me. This book will take you through twenty-one days of looking on the inside and what I experienced to find love within.

# DAY 1: Created from the Inside

*"My frame was not hidden from You, When I was made in secret, And skillfully wrought in the depths of the earth."*
~ *Psalm 139:15 (New American Standard Bible)*

It is amazing how much God loves us. Can you imagine that, while you were being formed in the womb of your mother, you already had a purpose? Your life was already designed and fashioned to be great. You see, He shaped us first on the inside. He knew, on the inside, I had to be molded. He had to set a fire and a desire on the inside of me, that desire to praise and worship Him. You see, on the inside, He designed you to be fearfully and wonderfully made. On the inside, He shaped your destiny. He shaped your worth. It all started on the inside. God wanted the best, and everything He created was good. As He watched you in the womb, He watched you being formed. He protected you on the inside. He knew what He was doing when He created you on the inside. He had it all planned out. He never abandoned you;

instead He gave you a love you could depend on. Wow! How about that? How do you feel about that? So then out of the womb, you were formed. Out came a breathtaking, sculpted life from nothing to something, and He said, you were marvelously made. What a creation on the inside. Like an open book, God knows everything about you. You cannot hide anything from Him because He foreknew you. The one thing I love about God is He knows me. I cannot hide anything from Him. The Bible says, "Because he hath set his love upon me, therefore will I deliver him: I will set him on high, because he hath known my name" (Psalms 91:14 King James Bible).

You know, as a teenager, I didn't know who I was. I made a lot of mistakes because I didn't know me. I came from a loving family, and all was well, but I was lost. I was not in touch with me. You see, I put everything and everybody before me. Why? Because I didn't know me. God had sculpted this wonderful being. But there was a me who didn't know me. I was looking for love in all the wrong places. Not knowing it was inside of me. You see, when God was watching me grow from conception, He was preparing me to love me. He had already prepared my heart to love me on the inside. But what happened? I didn't know the truth about who I was. In this book Looking for Love in all the Right Places, it is important that we focus on the love that God has created within our hearts. This first lesson is so important because this is the beginning of you finding the real you. It is important that you reflect on the sculpted being that has been transformed into a wonderful creation — You! It begins on the inside. So let's take a further look at the inside of you. There are developmental stages after you are created on the inside. Out of the womb, you are that force to be reckoned with. But the stages to getting there are a process. When you were born in that womb, you were unaware of any separateness from your mother. You and your mother were one. You began to realize you had hands. You also began to trust in the one who cared for you to satisfy your needs. After a time, the process of you developing continued. You became aware of the differences between you and others. Then you bonded with those around you. It is important, as a teen or as a young woman, that you accept who you are. You are you. You might be black, white, or Hispanic, but it does not matter. All that matters is who you are. The color of your skin does not make you any better than anyone else. The same thing goes for the color of your hair, your eyes. Remember, the Creator watched over you in the womb. He knew everything about you, and it was good. So, repeat after me, "God created me, and it was good!"

Let me describe what looking for love in all the right places looks like. It means you no longer search for that love. Most of the time, people are searching for someone who will complete them or for someone who will affirm them. So what you have to do is learn to love yourself. Self-love is so important because, once you love yourself and treat yourself good, you learn not to settle for less. When you know you deserve the best, you have to get to know you and accept you for who you are and who God created you to be. It is time to get to know you. It is time to date you. When you start looking for love in all the right places, you start living a life that is designed for you. You are no longer following someone's else dream or path; you are now on your own dream or path because you are learning to love you. You know what you need and want. Looking for love in all the right places means you are learning to do what is right for you. I just want to be me. I am taking off the masks. I am no longer concerned about what you think about me. I love me. And I embrace who I am. So if I want to change me, it is to please me, not to please anyone else. My thinking is different. I want you to know, just as a butterfly is designed by God to soar, so are you! However, the butterfly can only emerge in its beautiful color and magnificent wings after it has been transformed within the warm cocoon of its Creator! You have to love you. You must be devoted to you. That is why, in this book, you will find daily affirmations that you can say about you. Practice saying them every day. Be good to you. If you don't treat yourself well, how can you expect someone else to? Last but not least, I know I am loved by a man who will never leave me or forsake me. His name is Jesus. He loves me unconditionally. If He thought to love me, then I must think enough to love me. You are the right place to look for love. "It is inside of you."

**Affirmations:**

I was created in His image.

I'm wonderfully and fearfully made.

I am in love with me.

I am in love with God.

**Prayer:** Father, I thank you. You have created me in Your image and after Your likeness. I thank You and accept that I am fearfully and wonderfully made. You formed and shaped me while I was in my mother's womb. You have created me for Your glory. You have created me with purpose. You have created me with Your love. Now, teach me how to love myself the way You love me. Let me experience the love You have placed on the inside of me, so I may receive love from others. Amen.

## DAY 2: His Plan for Me

*"For I know the plans I have for you," declares the LORD, "plans to prosper you and not to harm you, plans to give you hope and a future." ~ Jeremiah 29:11(New International Version)*

Praise the Lord! It is a blessing to know that our Father in Heaven has the blueprint for our lives. He knows everything we need. He has gone through our lives and laid out a good life for us because, the truth is, He loves us. Every detail, every thought, every care was planned for you. The color of your skin, your shape, the color of your eyes. You see, God has a plan. He designed you just to be you. When we think about His plan to prosper you, He is saying, "Daughter, I want you to flourish and thrive, to become a woman who knows who you are in Him. I want you to grow in me."

Think about that for a minute. I want you to really process that thought in your mind. God wants to prosper you. Do you know of anyone that has ever said that to you? No, because no one loves you like He does. His plan is to make sure that your life is complete in Him. That is why it is important that you are looking for love in all the right places. You see, the ultimate sacrifice was for you to become the best that you can be in Him. It is important to know the Master Planner. To know the plan God has for you, you must accept Him as your personal savior and make Him Lord of your life. You see you are only going to know the plan when you get to know Him. I know some of you reading this book have had a boyfriend or husband. Question: How did you get to know him? By spending time with him, right? So if you want to know the plans God has for you and if you want to know what they are, you must be in the right relationship with Him. When I first read this scripture, something just jumped out at me. My God has plans to prosper me, not to harm me, and He has plans to give me hope and a future. You know I really wished I had known this in my early years. You see, I went to church every Sunday when I was growing up. I was even the first youth minister at my church at the age of sixteen. Yes, I was in church, but I did not truly know all God had planned for me. I made so many mistakes because I didn't know His plan. I looked for love in all the wrong places. The most important thing that you must know is that God has already gone through your life and laid everything out for you. He has prepared the way through Jesus the Christ. I know we get caught up in the hype, wanting to feel wanted and loved, so we forget who we are. I want you to know how much God loves you! He has something great in store for you. The plan was so well thought out. As I close the lesson for today, just know that God's plan for you is not evil. He will never hurt you. He will never leave you. He will always be there for you. He will always comfort you. No matter what you are going through or have been through, He will always protect you. So just know that your future is bright.

**Affirmations:**

I am in love with me.

I am in love with God.

I am complete in Him.

I am a designer original.

**Prayer:** Father, I thank you for adding me in your plan. I thank you for promising to take care of me. God, thank you for having my life all planned out—plans to take care of me, not to abandon me, plans to give me eternal life. But most of all, God, you have promised to love me always. Amen.

## Day 3: Created in Christ

*"For we are his workmanship, created in Christ Jesus unto good works, which God hath before ordained that we should walk in them."* ~ *Ephesians 2:10 (King James Bible)*

My mind is racing because I am sitting here in awe of my God. I am thinking about God and how I am His workmanship, His masterpiece, but it doesn't stop there. You were created in Christ Jesus unto Good Works. You know God is awesome. There are so many young women who don't know what they were created for. They have allowed the world to make them think they are nothing. They have allowed situations to set them back, and they are stuck in a cycle of hurt, pain, and abuse. You see, not knowing why you were created is the reason for all of this. Repeat after me, "I belong to God. I am His gift." I want you to really get that in your spirit. Think about it for a minute. When I was in my early years, I had no clue as to who, what, when, where, and how. You see, I was bullied in school a lot. The girls didn't accept me for the color of my skin, so I was rejected by my peers. Looking back, I can remember one day walking in the cafeteria, and as I was coming through the door, a girl looked at me and said, "Why are you coming in here?" You know, she always tried to intimidate me. At that time, I walked in fear, so I walked out of the cafeteria. I am saying this to let you know that you cannot let people make you feel inadequate. If only you knew how much God put into you to make you His designer original, then you would know and act like there is no one like you. You are unique, and because of that, you need to pick yourself up and go, girl. You must value you. You must know that God did not make a mistake. No matter who your mother or father is, you are here on this earth for a reason. And because of that, you must know God took the time to make sure you would be here on this earth, and that means a lot. It doesn't matter who likes you. Are you not keeping it moving because God has a job for you to do on this earth for Him? After learning all of this, I forgave that girl who bullied me in school. I forgave her because she did not know she was a masterpiece, as well, who God had designed for greatness. You must know that your life has a meaning. The Master Builder made sure of that, so you can't let anyone stop you from accomplishing anything you want to do because your God is right there with you, seeing that what He created is and will be the best. You are a masterpiece. Well, what is a masterpiece? A work of outstanding artistry, skill, or workmanship, a work done with extraordinary skill, especially of supreme intellectual or artistic achievement (Merriam-Webster's Dictionary). God is at the base of your creation, and that means you are a masterpiece. You were made with skill and achievement, so look within yourself and tell yourself, "I was created for greatness."

**Affirmations:**

I am a masterpiece.

I am extraordinary.

I am in love with me.

I am in love with God.

**Prayer:** Father, in the name of Jesus, I am so grateful that you have showered me with your grace and kindness. Thank you, Lord, for setting the example that I must live by. Thank you, God, for helping me demonstrate a life of gratitude and character. Father, thank you for touching my heart and opening my eyes, so I can see the work of art that I have become. Amen.

# Day 4: My Heart Trusts Him

*"Trust in the Lord with all thine heart; and lean not unto thine own understanding. In all thy ways acknowledge him, and he shall direct thy paths." ~ Proverbs 3:5-6 (King James Bible)*

Trusting God is having an assurance in Him. Having an assurance in Him is saying, "I am guaranteed, and I know for sure that, whatever His word has said about me, I will believe it." We all have faced disappointments in life. That has caused us to shut down and depend on the wrong things. But God wants you to know how much He loves you. You can put your trust in Him and never ever be let down. We go wrong when we put our trust where there is no guarantee for love, just hurt and pain. I, for one, know what it is like to trust another with my heart. I mean, we are so weak when it comes to relationships and believing what someone says to us. That is the problem right there. We believe what they say and not what they do. God is a God of action. He backs up what He says. He will always come through for you. He is just waiting for you to trust Him. God tells us to "trust in Him with all thine heart. And lean not unto thine own understanding" (Proverbs 3:5-6 King James Bible). When we lean on our own understanding, we trust our own information that we have obtained from our intellect. That's leaning on your own understanding. Well, at one time, I was so messed up because I leaned on my own understanding. If a man told me he loved me, I trusted that without actions. All he had to do was whisper sweet nothings in my ear, and that was it. I was all in love, but it was not love at all.

We, as women, must trust our God with everything. We must know that, if He tells us to trust Him, we must trust Him. He is a God that is not going to fail us. He created us. He knows what we need. But when we are looking for love in all the wrong places, instead of in God, we are just setting ourselves up for failure. We must know that we must listen to the voice of God. Well, you might not know how to listen to His voice. Well, yes, you do. Just trust in the Word, pray, and ask Him to lead and guide you. You see, when we trust God, He will keep you on track. You must understand that we don't know it all. But we have a Father who does. Again, He has the blueprint for our lives. He knows our husband. He knows our children. He knows everything before we do, so, if we get ahead of Him and do not trust Him, we will get into something that is not of God. God wants the best for us. We must run to God and trust Him with every situation. You know, I can talk to Him about anything. And I never have to worry about it going anywhere. I never have to worry about Him telling my business because I trust Him. He will never hurt me or betray me. I believe trust is the greatest gift we can give God. When you are looking for love in all the right places, I think our minds tell us we have everything in control and we don't need to trust God. Well, there you have the problem. Give your will over to God. Trust Him with the plans.

**Affirmations:**

I am listening for His voice.

I am in love with me.

I am in love with God.

**Prayer:** Father, in the name of Jesus, thank you for teaching me to take to heart your commands. Lord, I know I cannot figure everything out on my own. But I trust you from the bottom of my heart. I know, Lord, that you will keep me on track, if I trust you. I give you my life today, and I trust you with all my heart. Please take out all fear and worry and let me allow you to take full control of my life. Amen.

# Day 5: We All Want to be Happy

*"Happy is that people, that is in such a case: yea, happy is that people, whose God is the Lord." ~ Psalm 144:15 (King James Bible)*

We all want to be happy, but sometimes trying to find happiness can be a struggle. Often, we search for it in all the wrong places or ways, when the answer is much simpler—God. "Happy [are] the people…whose God is the Lord," states Psalm 144:15 (King James Bible). Let's define happiness. Basically, it is the state of being happy. It means you are content with you. You enjoy you. I think the biggest problems with people is that they are not content with themselves. Again, going back to society and the world, we have always wanted to be somebody else or look like somebody else. But we are not them. We can only walk in our shoes. Our lives have been designed for us, not for someone else. So let's look to the Lord and find the happiness that we need. It is a choice. If you choose to be happy, you will be. You must command your day.

Tell yourself, "I am going to have a good day. No matter what comes my way, I am going to embrace this day and love me. I know things are going to come up, but I can handle them. God is in control, and if I trust in Him, He will and can work it out for me."

All you must do is have faith and believe, so tell yourself, "My happiness is in God, not people, places, or things." When your mindset is that way, your thoughts become positive. Even when a situation comes up, you can say, "God's got this." So today is the day that we remain happy in Him.

## Affirmations:

I am happy with me.

I am content with me.

I am in love with me.

I am in love with God.

**Prayer:** Father, in the name of Jesus, thank you for allowing me to know that my happiness is in you.

Lord, thank you. I am alive and complete in you. Lord, thank you for being the joy of my strength. Amen.

**Empowering Moment:**

As we are looking for love in all the right places? I can't say it enough. We must listen to the voice of God. When you listen to the voice of God, you are better able to help yourself and others. You also are being guided by the Holy Spirit by listening and doing what He is telling you to do. When you listen to Him, you are making the right decisions for your life. Your life depends on you making the right decisions. Here are a few steps to help you hear the voice of God:

1. Accept Him as Lord and Savior/Filled with the Holy Ghost
2. Fast and pray
3. Read the Word daily
4. Learn to drown out the noise of your daily routine! Example: Keep worship music playing in your home and in your car. If you can, put

your earphones in at work. That is, only if your employer allows you to.

5. Attend church and Bible study regularly
6. Surround yourself with positive people who will speak life and hold you accountable.

# Day 6: Are You Loving the One You're With?

*"You shall love the Lord your God with all your heart and with all your soul and with all your might."* ~ *Deuteronomy 6:5 (New American Standard Bible)*

Are you loving the one you are with? You might think I am talking about a spouse, boyfriend, or whoever you are with, but, no, I am asking, are you loving you? Think about this...You are with you twenty-four hours a day, every day. There is no one that is with you all those hours but you. So again, are you loving the one you are with? We are looking at the fact of you loving you. You must also ask yourself, Do I want to love me? Well, you should. I have wondered about "me loving me." It seems we get caught up in the day-to-day life of being busy and doing for others, and that is great, but what about you? Are you taking care of you? Are you giving yourself the proper care that you need to go forward and continue to live?

My mind needs to be stimulated. My heart needs to be regulated. My soul needs to be filled, and my body needs to be nourished. Let's look at the mind. We want to deal with your thoughts. What do you think about you? Yes, answer the question. You love your boo. You have great thoughts of him or her, so tell me, when you think about you, what do you think? Or do you think about you? That is a good question. Well, I can tell you, at one time, I didn't think about me. I am being honest. I was so wrapped up into everything and everybody else. I didn't ever matter. I felt like a robot. Do you know how a robot feels? I was programed to do this, do that for everyone else until I did nothing constructive for me. My thoughts about me were irrelevant. I had lost my desire to love me. You might think, What? Yes, at one point, I felt very low about myself. Even though I was masking it and smiling and working and doing for everybody else, I neglected me. So, if I neglected me, who else do you think I neglected? Yes, God. I neglected my relationship with God because I was so busy. And my mind was on pleasing people. Thank God for deliverance, and when

I got hold of Romans 12: 1-2, let me tell you…I was set free. I had to do something. I had to order my life. I had to repent and present. Yes, that rhymes. But I had to ask God to forgive me for not taking care of me, for not taking care of this temple that He had so blessed me with. I had to go before Him and cry out to Him because my mind was full of crazy things. Unfortunately, they were not the right things. And I decided to renew my mind. It took a lot of prayer. Why? Because when you are so used to doing something one way, it is hard to change. So this is the order in which I have rearranged my life. God is first. I am second, and what I can do, I will do. So, yes, I think about me. Writing this, I am sad. I feel bad about the things I did to me. But God has forgiven me. And it is okay. Looking for love in all the right places means I am loving God first and loving me is okay. I also love my neighbor, and it is not about me pleasing my neighbor but really loving them.

**Affirmations:**

I am forgiven for not loving me.

I am in love with me.

I am in love with God.

**Prayer:** Father, I thank You for forgiving me for the way I neglected myself. Lord, I thank You because, through it all, you gave me the opportunity, through Your son, to love again. Lord, I ask You, in the name of Jesus, to continue to shine Your love on me and through me, so I can show others how to love.

# Day 7: I am Worth the Wait

*"Who can find a virtuous woman? For her price is far above rubies."* ~ *Proverbs 31:10*
*(King James Version)*

There is a saying: "When you are tempted to compromise your values because of how you feel, remind yourself, 'I am worth the wait.'" That has happened to a lot of young girls and women.

They have compromised their values, lowered their standards to find love or settled for whatever came their way, even when it was not love. I believe we, as women, do an injustice to ourselves when we just settle for anything, just to say we have someone. Looking for love in all the right places override a settler. Now you are a believer in you. When you believe in you, you know your purpose. You know why you are here. You tell yourself, "I am worth the wait. I am worth me taking care of me. I am worth me loving me. I'm worth you taking your time with me and not rushing me."

Was it a hard task for me to affirm me and what was best for me? Well, yes, it was. So, trust me, I understand. When you are putting your life into perspective and setting things in order, it is difficult, sometimes, for us to see and know what is really best for us because we are so used to things. The scripture for today asks the question, "Who can find a virtuous woman?" You may be wondering, what is a virtuous woman? A virtuous woman is a woman who knows her worth. The next question is, "Who can find one?" I believe the woman who is reading this book has just found out who she really is. Don't get me wrong. You may not feel like it, but I want you to know you are that woman of worth, that woman of standard. You are that woman who is loved by an almighty God. Life can deal us a hand that might be hard to bear. But God is there. We have all made mistakes. We have all felt like we have failed, but even in that, you are still a standing woman of God, and He wants to use you. In this lesson,

I want you to take a piece of paper and answer the following questions:

1. What is my purpose?
2. Why am I here?
3. Where am I going? Where do I see myself in five years?
4. How am I going to get there?

These are just a few questions that need to be answered by you. Only you know you and what you want. The end of the scripture says, "Her price is far above rubies." Wow! What a powerful woman. Looking at this woman, the Proverbs 31 woman, I see a very confident woman who knows what she needs, not just what she wants. Waiting on God can, sometimes, be a challenge because you get desperate and you start going to other sources for help, especially if you feel God is not moving fast enough because we want what we want right now. We must realize that waiting is where we really find God. Waiting is where we seize the moment to say, "God, I trust you. You are my source. You are my everything." Looking for love in all the right places is where we wait.

## Affirmations:

I am the expression of Christ.

I am in love with me.

I am in love with God.

**Prayer:** Father, thank You for making me in Your image. Thank You for making me a woman of worth. Father, thank You for making me the apple of Your eye. Amen.

# Day 8: Holiness

*"I beseech you therefore, brethren, by the mercies of God, that ye present your bodies a living sacrifice, holy, acceptable unto God, which is your reasonable service."* ~ Romans 12:1 (King James Bible)

Looking for love in all the right places…I have been thinking about the title, and it feels so good to look for love within me and find it. I am so excited about that. I can truly say, "I love me." But the key to all of this is Jesus. He is the one who gets all the glory. He gets the credit for this change in my life. You know, looking back on my early years, I lived to please the flesh. The flesh wanted what it wanted, and I gave into it. I had no idea what it meant to present my body as a living sacrifice. No wonder I was so messed up. You know, I want everyone who is reading this book to hear me loud and clear. You must come out of the darkness and go into the light. You must understand and know how much God wants the best for you, but you have to want the best for you, too. Holiness is defined as the state of being holy; purity or integrity of moral character, freedom from sin, sanctity (Webster's Dictionary 1828). Wow! Let's go. You got to be holy! Really! Yes, my friend, holiness is the way we as women should be. You see, we have lived for the world for so long until some of you don't want to come out of the sin. It has been imbedded in you. Trust me. I know. I've sinned…Okay, I admit it. I am not perfect. I was out there doing anything I was big or bad enough to do. Me being holy? There was no such thing. Me being pure? Right. Well, the devil told me those lies, told me I was nothing, was never going to be anything, and I fell for that lie. So much of my life has been wasted because I was practicing sin, but, God, I thank you for bringing me to the point of repentance that brought me to Holiness, so, when I think about Holiness, I don't think that I am holier than thou. I think of me wanting God to use me, so, if I wanted God to use me, I had to clean up my life. There are things I don't do anymore, places I don't go because I am presenting my body and my life as a living sacrifice. I want the Holy Ghost living on the inside. I want to look for love in me. Why?

Because God is on the inside. He lives in me, so I must carry myself as a child of the King of Kings because the one who has me living and breathing is in me, but I don't walk around in all white because it is not about the clothes I wear. It is about how I present my life to God. As I am writing this, I feel the presence of the Holy Ghost, so I pray, "God, I am so sorry for all the things I have done wrong in this body. For the person that is reading this, please work on them, like You did me. I give my life to You, Lord. Use me for Your service. Take out all the wrong and make me right before You."

I am sorry to you, who are reading this, the presence of God is in this room. Please wherever you are, just bow before Him and ask Him to do a new thing in your life. He loves you. He wants to work a miracle in you. No matter what you have done or where you have been, God loves you.

## Affirmations:

I am a new creation in Christ Jesus.

I am in love with me.

I am in love with God.

**Prayer:** Father, in the name of Jesus, You are a holy God, and I desire to be holy and set apart unto You. So, Lord, help me live my life in a manner that is pleasing to You. Amen.

## Day 9: Living a Life of Freedom

*"If the Son therefore shall make you free, ye shall be free indeed." ~ John 8:36 (King James Bible)*

Freedom. No more shackles. No more chains. No more bondage. I am free. Yes, I love it. God has made us free. When you are looking for love in all the right places, it feels good to know that you can be free to love God, free to love yourself, free to love others, free to love everybody. As I am writing this, I am inspired by God to bring you everything He is telling me to write. You see, I gave up my plan, and this book is His plan, so I must listen to the one who has the plan. I am free to give my will over to Him and trust that He knows what He is doing. I don't, so I am free to give it over to Him. Freedom is a choice. You see, we are no longer in bondage because of the blood that was shed on Calvary. Jesus did everything He was assigned on this earth to do, so we could be free. It is around 5:22 in the morning, and I have to shout and praise my God. Let me tell you something, if you are in a situation and you don't want to be in it, get out. If someone is hurting you, making you feel uncomfortable, get out. You don't have to stay in a situation that is causing you pain and heartache; you are already free, but you must trust and believe that you are. Jesus paid a price for your freedom, so take advantage of that. Living a free life is liberating. I mean, you don't carry those weights on your shoulders. I have been so happy since I allowed myself to understand the meaning of my freedom. I started living life as a free woman, not as a bound woman. You, too, can start living your life as a woman with no chains. This was how we looked in the past. Have you ever seen a prisoner bound in chains? Well, that was what we looked like in the spirit when Jesus said, "I tell you most solemnly that anyone who chooses a life of sin is trapped in a dead-end life and is, in fact, a slave" (John 8:34-38 The Message [MSG]). A slave is a transient who can't come and go at will. The Son, though, has an established position, the run of the house, so, if the Son sets you free, you are free through and through. Praise God! We are no longer in bondage to the world. We are now looking for love in all the right places and finding love within. Don't you feel good about yourself? Don't you know how much God truly loves you? Do you know the extent of what He went through just, so you could live the good life? So today is a day that you can look in the mirror and tell yourself, "I am free." But you must want to be free. So please allow God to love on you. If a man or woman is hurting you, that is not love. That is manipulation and control. God wants you to be safe and secure in Him, so trust Him with your life today. We are no longer slaves to this world or to man. We are free.

**Affirmations:**

I am free because of God.

I am in love with me.

I am in love with God.

**Prayer:** Father, I come to you now in the name of Jesus, thanking you for the precious blood of Jesus. I present myself to you. By the power of His shed blood, I bind the power of Satan's demons and all dominion of darkness seeking entrance into my life. I receive the freedom to live as you intended, in Jesus's name. Amen.

# Day 10: His Love is Unconditional

*"The LORD has appeared of old unto me, saying, Yea, I have loved you with an everlasting love: therefore with lovingkindness have I drawn you." ~ Jeremiah 31:3 (King James 2000 Bible)*

When you are looking for love in all the right places, one of the most important things is to accept the fact that God loves you. But to do that, you must accept Him as your personal savior and make Him Lord of your life. So, what do you do when you accept something? You receive it. So, what stops me from accepting His love? We live in a very cruel world. People have hurt us. And we feel that we cannot trust. You feel you cannot trust God. The one thing about God is, when He says something, He means it. He will not go back on His word. God wants to be the God of every man and woman, boy and girl. He wants to call us His own. He will always love us. Well, I have decided that, according to Proverbs 3:5-6 (King James Bible): "Trust in the LORD with all thine heart; and lean not unto thine own understanding. In all thy ways acknowledge him and he shall direct thy paths." He's the one who will keep you on track. Wow! Enough said. The Bible clearly states that I must trust God "with all thine heart." And when I do, He will keep me on track. Knowing that God loves me even when I mess up is amazing. Really God is aware of all my flaws. It is good to know that He looks beyond our faults and sees our needs. You see, God knows we need love. We were created to love and to be loved. God told them, "I've never quit loving you and never will. Expect love, love, and more love!" Jeremiah 31:2-6 (The Message [MSG]). God's love will never let us down.

**Affirmation:**

I am loved by the best.

**Prayer:** Father, in the name of Jesus, thank you for loving me even when I don't love myself. When the scripture says, "His love in unfailing," that is what it means. Unfailing is certain, dependable, and trustworthy. The most important thing I have realized about His love is that it is constant. That means, no matter what I do, no matter where I go, His love for me will always be there for me. What is it going to take for you to realize that our Master has love for you and will never stop loving you? What I want you to do is to know that this everlasting love that God has for you reaches to the depth of your soul, your mind, and your body. Because of this everlasting love, you should never ever feel unloved ever again. When you are faced with the fact that you believe no one loves you, it is plain that God does and He will never stop. Have you ever felt drawn to something, something that pulls you in a direction that you just don't understand? When that happens, stop and pay attention. That is the hand of God drawing you to Him. So just know, He is going to get your attention one way or another. Choose His love today.

**Affirmations:**

I am loved with an everlasting love.

I am in love with me.

I am in love with God.

**Prayer:** Father, in the name of Jesus, thank you for your everlasting love. Thank you for your love that reaches to the depth of my soul and pulls me in to purpose. I thank you for loving me. Amen.

# Day 11: Love Never Fails

*"Love never fails. But whether there be prophecies, they will fail; whether there be tongues, they will cease; whether there be knowledge, it shall vanish away." ~ 1Corinthians 13:8 (King James 2000 Bible)*

When it looks like it's real, but it's not...Have you ever been in love before? Most of us have. And most of us have experienced what we thought was love when it was really lust. Wow! So real. Yes, let's keep it real. We are living in a day when love is given, and love is taken. People say, "I love you" all the time, just to get what they want. They will use you for their purpose to get what they want. Young girls often fall for the "I love you" line. And it is taken literally...I am sending a message to you to help you understand that love will never fail you.

Here is an example. Mary met Paul, and they started to date. She was saving herself for her husband because she really wanted to walk down the aisle a virgin on her wedding day. When she told him that she was waiting, at first, he said, "Okay. I understand." They kept dating, and then one night while they were out, he told her how much he loved her, how much he really wanted to spend the rest of his life with her, so they went back to his place, and it happened. She gave herself to him, thinking that this would be the one she would spend the rest of her life with. Afterward, however, he stopped calling. He didn't want to see her anymore. After this, Mary was in a state of depression because she felt betrayed and rejected, and she started to lose her zest for life. She quit school because she had no desire to live. During all of this, she got involved with the wrong crowd and became very wild and crazy. Mary was like so many young girls who looked for love in all the wrong places. Mary felt like her life was over. Well, long story short, Mary went with her family to church, and that was what saved her. She went on a youth retreat and rededicated her life to Jesus. Today, Mary is doing great. She finished school, went off to college, and met the man God had ordained for her. The guy she met was so gentle. He loved her.

They dated for about six months. They did not have sex. He, too, was a Christian and wanted to please God with his body. But he loved Mary with everything, so they were married and have six beautiful children. In Mary's early years, she was broken and shattered, but the love of God came in and healed all her wounds. God's love is amazing. You see, that experience caused Mary to understand the importance of loving herself. That one experience caused her to think differently about her life and what she needed to do. She made up her mind, after that youth retreat, that her life mattered and, most of all, that His love would never fail her, so we see a woman who decided that she would not let another man steal her heart because she had already given her heart to Jesus, and He gave her a brand-new life. Praise God!

**Affirmations:**

I am reconciled to God.

I am what I am.

I am in love with me.

I am in love with God.

**Prayer:** Father, in the Name of Jesus, I thank you for looking beyond my faults and seeing my needs. Thank you, Lord, for your love that never fails. Amen.

# Day 12: My Knight in Shining Armor

*"God is bedrock under my feet, the castle in which I live, my rescuing knight. My God — the high crag where I run for dear life, hiding behind the boulders, safe in the granite hideout." ~ Psalm 18:2 (The Message [MSG])*

Every woman is looking for her knight in shining armor to come and rescue her and save her. Well, what if he never comes? What if you get so caught up in looking for love in the all the wrong places that you miss him? That's the mindset of every girl and woman. I used to feel that way. It seemed like I was always looking for him. I thought every man that smiled was him! Yes, I can admit that I was desperate. I am going to be real in this book about the things I experienced. I am not ashamed because, since then, God has delivered me. Yes, at times, it can be so disheartening because you are constantly wanting to be loved by somebody. I know I have talked to numerous girls, and that's what they have said, "We just want to be loved." I understand the feeling. I understand their hearts and your heart. That is why this book is so important for you to go through and be encouraged. Once, I was just like you. Once, I was one of those women who did look for love in all the wrong places. But now, since I have fallen in love with Jesus, I now look for love in all the right places. The right place for me was when I realized that my knight in shining armor had already come. He had always been there. Let me introduce you to my man. His name is JESUS! I am going to be straight up with you. I didn't always know He was there. I wasn't looking for love from Jesus; I was looking for love from a man. Come on! There are some beautiful creations out there. Even so, they could not love me and do for me like my true knight in shining armor could. You see, after I realized how much God truly loved me, I changed my perspective. I stopped thinking about a man, and I started praying to God for Him to find me. You see, I stopped looking and started praying. And after a time, I said, "God, you are the one. If a man wants me, He must go to you."

Now, I have come to grips with me. Through failed relationships and marriages, I was not just the other person. It was time to look in the mirror and say, "God, I surrender my life to you." When you are looking for love in all the right places and when you find love within, you realize that you have a fervent love for God. Look at David in the passage, He is letting God know that he is His rock. He is saying, "God, You are my rock. I can depend on you." We, as women, must understand that our knight in shining armor is our provider, our healer, and our deliverer. He is our everything. One thing that I know for sure is He will come to my rescue.

**Affirmations:**

I am accepted by the beloved.

I am in love with me.

I am in love with God.

I am alive with Christ.

**Prayer:** Father, thank You for being the vine because I am the branch living in You. Thank You, Lord, for hiding me under the shadow of Your wing. Lord, I trust in You. Amen.

# Day 13: Devoted Confidence

*"I can do all things through Christ who Strengthens me."*
*~ Philippians 4:13 (King James 2000 Bible)*

Praise the Lord when you are that confident woman, when you are a woman who is sure of what she wants to do or needs to do. There are times in our lives that things do come up. There are things in our past that try to push us back, but one thing you must remember is that God is right there with you, and He will never leave you or forsake you. Let me tell you this. I have been through so much in my life. I am just going to keep it real. There are things that I am not happy about. But I must stay true to what God has called me to do. For me to remain confident in who I am and my God, I have to stay devoted to Him. I have had to pick myself up when I didn't want to. I used to think, There is so much against me, but the Word says, "If God is for us, who can be against us?" (Romans 8:31 New International Version). I knew those forces that kept trying to make me feel that I was nothing. Those things being whispered in my mind tried to take me out. What did I do? I stood on the Rock, the Rock that is higher than me. I am shouting unto the Lord because today I am that confident woman. I know who I am. I know that God is for me. But I had to be for Him. I had to give up all the things that tried to set me back, so devoted confidence is not just in you, it is in God. You see, the victory came when I decided not to cling to people or possessions. My hope is in Jesus. I had to commit my confidence in God, so was it that easy? Let me tell you, at first, it was a struggle. Why? Because I had to give up my agenda and let God be God. All He wanted me to do was totally surrender my life to Him. He wanted me to trust in Him. I was trusting in people and what I could do, but I didn't get a breakthrough until I totally gave it all to Jesus. Now, my mind says, "Yes, all this time, He was right there, waiting for me to say, 'God, I give it over to you.'"

"I have been crucified with Christ and I no longer live, but Christ lives in me. The life I now live in the body, I live by faith in the Son of God, who loved me and gave himself for me" (Galatians 2:20 New International Version). Praise Him! He gave Himself for me. Now, I am strong when I am weak. I can do all things through Christ because I am in His will and He empowers me to do it. For us to continue to be confident women, we must care. We must use this scripture as the anthem of our lives. "I (We) can do all things through Christ." I am sitting here, almost in tears, because I know the failures in my life happened when I was not doing things God's way, and because of that, I made some costly mistakes. I can't blame anyone but me. I don't want you to make those same mistakes. Pick yourself up, girls, and know that God loves you. Yes, you can do it.

**Affirmations:**

I am strong in the Lord.

I am confident to the end.

I am in love with me.

I am in love with God.

**Prayer:** Father, in the name of Jesus, thank You for making me a confident woman. Lord, it is in Your power and your might that You have made me who I am. God, thank You for sending Your word and it is what it says I am. Amen.

# Day 14: Moving Forward

*"If we confess our sins, he is faithful and just and will forgive us our sins and purify us from all unrighteousness."* ~ 1 John 1:9 (New International Version)

It is time to leave should've, would've, and could've behind! Say goodbye! It is time to move forward. We must begin the process of letting go of the things that have held us back today. It is time to say, "I have had enough." Your life has a new meaning, but you must be ready to forgive yourself and those who have hurt you. The pain, I know, can be severe, but you can do it. First, you don't need anyone's permission to move forward. It is time to say, "God, I trust you, and I believe that my life has moved ahead." If not, you will remain stuck in that place of fear, doubt, and uncertainty. Define forgiveness as "the act of pardoning an offender." In the Bible, the Greek word for forgiveness literally means "to let go." Jesus used the following explanation when He taught His followers to pray: "Forgive us our sins, for we ourselves forgive everyone who is indebted to us" (Luke 11:4 English Standard Version). I think this says it all. Let it go. I truly believe that, when you don't forgive, the person holds power over you. When you are looking for love in all the right places, forgiveness says, "I am bigger than this. Because you have hurt me, I am still going to love you. And because I love you, I also love myself, so I must let it go."

Forgiveness brings about freedom and relief. I know how it is to have someone hurt you and to see that person and you basically must smile and keep it moving. But I know I could not keep avoiding the issue, so I went to the person, and I said, "I am sorry if I offended you." Well, I didn't offend the person; they had offended me. I knew this person was not going to ever say anything to me because of pride. I had to free myself. After I said what I said, the other person started crying and begged for forgiveness because they knew they had hurt me. After the reconciliation, we both were able to move forward. When we see each other today, we have the utmost respect for one another. No more excuses about why you can't, so let's say, "I can." God has given you the power to love and forgive. When He was hanging on the cross, He said, "Father, forgive them; for they know not what they do" (Luke 23:34 King James Bible). So here we see our Savior forgiving those who hurt Him. We must do this, too.

**Affirmations:**

I am not bound by the past.

I am in love with me.

I am being changed in His image.

I am in love with God.

**Prayer:** Father, please forgive us for holding on to those things of the past. Thank you for washing us and making us new.

Empowering Moment: Life is what you make it, so you must decide how you want to live your life. You must know that you were fearfully and wonderfully made. You were created in the image of God. There is greatness inside of you. Don't ever let anyone tell you that it is not. You see, the devil does not like us. He hates us. He wants us to fail. But God loves us and His plan for us is to succeed. So, on this day, just know that you can do all things through Christ. There is nothing that you can't accomplish, nothing that you can't do. But you must renew your mind. You must believe in the God you serve. You must believe in you. Believe in you today. Just know life is what you make it. God already made it.

# Day 15: Listening in the Right Place

*"My sheep hear My voice, and I know them, and they follow Me." ~ John 10:27 (King James Bible)*

As we are beginning our journey of looking for love in all the right places, we must know that we will come across some barriers and blocks that will try to get in our way. That's okay. It happens. But learning to listen is so important on this journey to finding love within. It is important, especially as the Word tells us to be swift to hear. Bottom line, just be quiet. We can open our mouths and say some of the craziest things because we are not following the Word or out of ignorance or just to say it, but as we are learning to listen, we can apply truth to our lives. We must submit and again just be quiet. We can look at the blocks that can cause us not to listen, especially when we know that we have too many distractions or are listening to the wrong voices. It is easy because, when you don't know how to listen to the voice of God, the first thing you do is go and ask someone what they think or what their opinion is, not what God wants. As we are looking for love in all the right places, we must know who is speaking and if it is the truth. Now, don't get me wrong. God has placed some people in our lives who really know exactly what to say and when. But I want you to get used to listening to the voice that lies within, and you can't go wrong when you do that. We must learn, as women, that God does speak to us. But if you are not listening, you will not hear what He has to say. Will He speak to you? Yes. How? In His word, through people, but He does speak audibly. For example, I was in a situation where I heard God speak to me, and I didn't listen. Trust me. I heard His voice. I heard the voice of God! He told me not to do something, but I did it anyway. Why yes, me. This was when I was about to get married. I don't mind sharing this because I wanted to be open with you. I thought I was in love with this man. I had been single and not dating for so many years. I was just starting my ministry, and things were going great. I had vowed that I was never going to get married because of the hurt and pain I had been through, so I had given up on men. I am not degrading men, but just for me, at that time, that was the way I was feeling, but I met this man, and he was really into God. He was a man of faith who really loved God. He wanted to date me, so I agreed. I told him we were going to do things according to the Word, so we abstained from any sexual involvement. I wanted to do this by the book, so we dated for a year. After the year, we set a date. On the day of the wedding, I had to go and pick up something for the wedding. While I was doing this, God spoke to me. He said, "If you believe that I speak audibly, don't marry this man." I said, "Okay. Whose voice is this?" The wedding was set. The guests had been invited, but a voice had spoken to me. What was I supposed to do? I was so happy and excited about this new husband I was about to marry. But the voice had said, "Don't marry this man." It's the devil, I thought.

Well, months later, this marriage turned out to be a lie. I was determined to make it work, so I stayed in all the hell I was going through, just for the sanctity of the marriage, but he left because he, too, knew his heart was not with me. So let me tell you something. Listening to God is so important. When God speaks, we must listen. You see, if I had set my emotions aside at that time and prayed and not worried about the wedding, I would have known it was God, so Jesus says, "My sheep know my voice" (John 10:27 Contemporary English Version). When He speaks to you, will you listen? Will you know His voice? When you are born again, you become His child, and because of that, He speaks to His children. Will you listen?

**Affirmations:**

I am following Christ.

I am in love with me.

I am born again.

I am in love with God.

**Prayer:** Father, help me to know Your voice. Train me to listen to and follow You for the rest of my days. Help me to know when You are speaking to me. Amen.

# Day 16: Master Yourself

*"If you do what is right, will you not be accepted? But if you do not do what is right, sin is crouching at your door; it desires to have you, but you must master it."* ~ Genesis 4:7 (New International Version)

I preached a sermon one time that was entitled "You Must Master You." In looking for love in all the right places, we must understand that love is on the inside. It has always been there. The only reason you have not known that is because you have not opened yourself to love you. I know, I know. You're wondering, what does that mean? Well, it means that you must accept who you are. I know we have grown up in situations that have caused us some hurt. Some of you have grown up in a single-family home. Some have had two parents and still lived in a dysfunctional home. But what I want you to see is this—no matter what, you must master you. You must understand that doing what is right is always the key to your success. It is the key to you finding love within. I talk to a lot of young girls, and they tell me, "I can't talk to my mom because she does not listen to me." So, because your mom does not listen to you, you are getting in trouble at school or showing no respect for yourself? I want you to now get rid of the excuses because the excuses that you are making do not justify you doing what you want to do. You must be accountable for your life. This is your life, and God has given you the opportunity to make the best out of your life. That is why I am writing this book, to help you understand that your life has meaning. You can't blame someone for your actions. You must take full responsibility for you, so, yes, mastering you is the key. If you don't, then as the scripture says, "Sin is crouching at your door" (Genesis 4:7 New International Version). Mastering sin is not a requirement to being loved by God. He knows that we will struggle and fall, sometimes, repeatedly. What He wants us to do, though, is walk with Him, see His ways, and grow as His children into mature daughters of Christ. Sin will always be lurking right outside our doors, but we all have the power to take control over it through a constant and steady relationship with the

Lord. If you want to look for love in all the right places, you must master you. You must get control of your emotions, your actions, and say, "I am going to do what is right with my life." God has given me this life, and I must, at all costs, show Him that I am grateful by giving Him my best. It is not hard to do. Just make up in your mind that doing what is right is what God requires of you. So I will say to you, "I am proud of you." I am glad that you decided to do what is right in the sight of God. He loves you and wants the best for you, but you must want the best for yourself.

**Affirmations:**

I accept me.

I am in love with me.

I am proud of me.

I am in love with God.

**Prayer:** Father, I thank You in the name of Jesus, for giving me the strength and the power to be an overcomer. Thank You for accepting me for who I am.

Thank You for Your love and compassion toward me. Amen.

# Day 17: To Love is to Obey

*"Jesus replied, 'Anyone who loves me will obey my teaching. My Father will love them, and we will come to them and make our home with them." ~ John 14:23 (New International Version)*

I truly believe that, when you make up your mind to obey God, you are saying, "I love You, and I am giving up everything to obey You." That is a powerful statement. When you love someone, you want to do everything in your power to please that person. You go out of your way to do things for that person, just to make sure they are happy. We can do the same thing in our lives. We must give it all up for the Master. John 14 says, "Anyone loves me will obey my teaching" (New International Version). So, you must ask yourself, "Do I love God?" I mean, you have to really think about this question. Do you really love God? Are you ready to give up your agenda to serve Him and do His will? As a woman, you must look in the mirror and make the choice. I mean, I can't make it for you. You must decide. I want you to live the good life. I want you to be successful. I want you to look for love within and find it. But you must decide if you want it. If you say, "Okay, I want to find this love within," then you must obey God. He knows what is best for you. He knows what you need. He has already gone through your life and laid out your life and put everything on your path for success, but in order to receive what the Father has for you, obedience is the key. I am writing this book from the heart. One of the most important things that I hope you get out of this book is that it is necessary to have "obedience to the Father." Please I implore you to take this seriously. You see, God wants your life to be what He created it to be — In His image. So, for your life to be in His image, you must want to be like Him. When He says not to do something, it is for a reason. Generally, it is because He wants to protect you from harm. When we don't do it His way, we are opening the door for the enemy to come in. For example, it is important to God that you live a pure and holy life. Yes, I am going to talk about sex. Why? Because so many young girls are looking for love in all the wrong places, as stated before. The Word tells us that we all have sinned and fallen short. We are not perfect; we are going to make mistakes. But in all of that, if we love God, we must obey Him. This is a story that my mom tells my sister and me. She learned this in Sunday school, and she says it has stuck with her. There was a woman who fell in love with this man and everyone told her to leave him alone, but she didn't. He left her and moved to another state. She got a package in the mail and opened it. It was a small casket, and in the inside of the casket, there was a note that read you are now dying. The guy had AIDS. So, you see, God said in 1 Corinthians 6:18-20 (New International Version): "Flee from sexual immorality. All other sins a person commits are outside the body, but whoever sins sexually sins against their own body. Do you not know that your bodies are temples of the Holy Spirit who is in you, who you have received from God? You are not your own; you were bought at a price. Therefore, honor God with your bodies." If you love Him, obey Him. Wait for your husband. His Word teaches us the truth. Because He is the truth. To obey Him is to love Him.

## Affirmations:

I am successful.

I am worth the wait.

I am in love with me.

I am in love with God.

**Prayer:** Father, in the name of Jesus, please forgive us for being disobedient to Your word. Please remove all rebellious spirts that would cause us not to obey You. We love You! Amen.

# Day 18: Making Peace with the Past

*"Peace I leave with you; my peace I give to you; I do not give to you as the world gives. Do not let your hears be troubled and do not be afraid."* ~ John 14:27 (New International Version)

You just must let it go! Easier said than done, I know. Yes, you can do it. When you are looking for love in the right places, are you looking for love in your past? I hope not. Are you looking for love within, from God? Your past is your past, and you cannot change it. The definition of "the past" is gone by in time and no longer existing. It no longer exists. It is gone. You can and must move on. I want to focus on a word that seems to be very important to every young girl and woman—SELF-ESTEEM. If you want to make peace with your past, then I believe you are on the road to having high self-esteem. The past is your history. The first thing is to let it go. If you want to hold on to the betrayal, the hurt, and the pain and just don't care, then I know you have low self-esteem. Again, we are down to a choice, I believe this, God cares for you. He loves you. He said he has left you His peace. Not as the world (hurt, pain abuse, unforgiveness, hate). He says he gave it to you. He said, "Let not your heart be troubled or let it be afraid." Come on now. We serve an awesome God! Today is the beginning of a fresh new start, so let's make the choice to walk out of the past and step into the future. I can remember attending a church in Maryland, and I went up to the altar for prayer. I was really going through something at the time, and I was really all emotional and feeling betrayed. I was visiting a new church, so the pastor did not know me. I stood in front of him. He said, "Woman of God, step up, then step back," so I did it. He said, "Step up and step back." He said, "When you step up the next time, I don't ever want you to look back." He said, "When you make this step forward, I want you to keep moving." I said, "Wow!" When I took that step forward, I let what was hindering me be left behind. Let me tell you, on that day after church, God released me from a bad situation never ever to go back into it again. I am so thankful for this pastor. I don't even know his name. All I know is God knew I was struggling, and He knew my heart was troubled. But after that day, God's peace came over me, and I let go of the past. Trust me. I tried to fight it. But God knew what was best for me. God does not want us walking around, looking back at something we cannot change. We, as women, must take care of ourselves and not allow the stress of life to get us down. Make peace with your past. Let it go, God has, and he no longer remembers your sins. He does not hold your past over your head to torment you and make you feel ashamed. What about you? Just a reminder while cleaning out the closest of past relationships and past hurts. Think about your relationship with yourself. How have you treated yourself? Have you loved yourself? Have you respected yourself? Ask yourself for forgiveness. That time is now. Find love within! It starts with you loving you.

**Affirmations:**

I forgive myself.

I am no longer holding myself hostage to the past.

I am in love with me.

I am in love with God.

**Prayer:** Father, in the name of Jesus, thank You for delivering me from my past. Father, I was created in Your image, and I thank You for not holding my past against me. Amen!

# Day 19: His Love is so Amazing

*"Ye have not chosen me, but I have chosen you, and ordained you, that ye should go and bring forth fruit, and that your fruit should remain: that whatsoever ye shall ask of the Father in my name, he may give it you." ~ John 15:16 (King James Bible)*

The thought of His love for us is so amazing. The fact that He chose us and ordained us, in all our mess, is so amazing. In everything we have down wrong, God (Yaweh) still loves us. He has appointed us to be His representatives here on earth, to go and preach and teach, to be change agents on this earth. So what is the problem? The world has a lot to offer. It has painted a pretty picture and made everything look so good, but the world has nothing to offer you but heartache and pain. We, as women, must know and realize who we are. We try to identify as and be someone else. We try and act like that person. We must try to mimic their ministry, try to look like them, to talk like them, dress like them. I want you to know the devil wants to steal your identity. He wants you to be something that you are not. You have a purpose for being born. There is a reason for your life. The tempter comes but for to steal. What? My life! He does not want us living the good life. Notice in the scripture John 10:10 (King James Bible): "The thief cometh not, but for to steal, and to kill, and to destroy: I am come that they might have life, and that they might have it more abundantly." Guess what. The devil does not love you. He will never love you, so what must we, as women, do to guard our hearts from the devil and stop being distracted from this enemy, especially when he tells us he loves us and will give us the world, and all the while, he is setting us up for a fall, in the same way he tried to tempt Jesus? We must do what Jesus did when he told him, "Get behind me, Satan. Man must not live by bread alone but by every word that proceeds out of the mouth of God." So yes, the Word is the Word. We must know the Word to keep our lives from being disappointed by the world. Let's back up a minute. You could say there are people in the world who know the world, and they are continuing to allow the devil to steal, kill, and destroy. The devil is doing his job. You must do yours. Knowledge is power, but the Bible says, "People perish from the lack of knowledge." Okay. What are we saying? For example, your employer tells you to not be late for work, but you continue to be late. What do you think is going to happen? You are going to get fired. If Jesus tells you that your body is the temple, but you continue to put all kinds of toxins in it, then what do you expect will happen? You see, we are free moral agents. We have the choice and the power…God has given us the power to say yes and the power to say no. So you choose this as your life. You must understand you are uniquely designed, and the devil does not like you. Your destination, after you leave this earth, is heaven. He knows that, so he is going to do everything he can to get and keep you off track. So make up in your mind that you are going to accept the love of God. He has prepared the good life for you. Remember, He has chosen you and ordained you. Go and bring fruit. Produce a harvest with your life.

**Affirmations:**

I am chosen by God.

I am ordained by God.

I am in love with me.

I am in love with God.

**Prayer:** Father, in the name of Jesus, thank You for sending your only son Jesus. Lord, thank You for choosing and appointing me to represent You. Lord, in the name of Jesus, my answer will always be yes. Thank You, God, for loving me. Amen.

# Day 20: I Am Made Whole

*"And he said unto her, Daughter, be of good comfort: thy faith hath made thee whole; go in peace." ~ Luke 8:48 (King James Bible)*

Looking for love in all the right places must be a goal that everyone seeks to find. You are a hidden treasure. You are a diamond in the rough. You are fearfully and wonderfully made, all the above. But you must know that. You must know that your faith is the key to your wholeness. As we look at this woman with the issue of blood, we see she had this issue for twelve long years. She sought all kinds of help from the world, but nothing could help her until she encountered Jesus. You see, Jesus is the answer for this world today. You see, looking at this woman, we see failure in man and success in Jesus. Why? Because our God is awesome, and He can do all things but fail. This woman with the issue of blood represents being an example for all women to see. When you put your trust in Jesus, He will not let you down. The woman with the issue of blood is someone I can relate to. She is someone that I can say, "Jesus, if You did it for her, I know You can do it for me. You healed her of her issues. Well, Jesus, we have some issues. Can You help us?" I know He would say, "Daughter, be of good comfort. Thy faith has made thee whole. Go in peace." That's the kind of God we serve. He is no respecter of person. He will do for us the same thing he did for the woman with the issue of blood, so what did she do? She stepped out on faith. She did not doubt that Jesus could heal her. As a matter of fact, she spoke her healing into existence before she touched Him. She declared and decreed a thing. And it was done. So what are you saying? What are you speaking about your life? God wants you to be whole. He does not want you all stressed out and worried. He does not want you sick. He came, so you could be well. The Bible says, in Matthew 9:29 (King James Bible), "according to your faith, be it unto you," so what do you want done unto you? The woman with the issue of blood wanted to be healed, regardless of what she had to do. You know, she could have been stoned or murdered because she was unclean. But God already knew his daughter was going to be used as a vessel of faith. We, too, must have faith to know that our God loves us, and He wants us whole. Looking for love in all the right places is all about being whole in our minds and bodies. You see, I was a young girl who was broken and shattered into many pieces. I was a doormat for so many people and was used and abused until I decided to step out on faith and believe in myself and love myself and know that love is within. I think back to the times I didn't feel loved. I felt like I was nothing, so I know what the woman with the issue of blood felt like. You see, I have low self-esteem problems. I really did. I had been hurt by so many people, even my own relatives. But like the woman with the issue of blood, I decided, one day, I had had enough, and I went to Jesus and He fixed me. He built up my faith. And know I was made whole. I don't care what people say about me anymore. I am predestined for greatness. I have been made whole.

**Affirmations:**

I am complete in Him.

I am a diamond in the rough.

I am in love with me.

I am in love with God.

**Prayer:** Father, in the name of Jesus, I thank you for healing and delivering me. Lord, when the enemy tried to keep me from you, thank you for giving me the strength and power to take that step of faith to find and experience real love. In Jesus's name. Amen.

# Day 21: No Self-Doubt

*"But when you ask, you must believe and not doubt, because the one who doubts is like a wave of the sea, blown and tossed by the wind." ~ James 1:6 (New International Version)*

I can tell you the devil tried to stop me from writing this book. He tried everything, saying, "You can't do it. No one will read it. You are a failure. No one cares about you." But I took my power back and said, "I will not doubt my ability to achieve again." You see, you must not have doubts because, if we doubt ourselves, we are unsure of ourselves. We are walking in fear and confusion. I mean, the list goes on and on. But if you are reading this book, I want to say first "thank you" for believing in me, and I pray, as you search for love, you find it in God and yourself. But I want to continue to reflect on self-doubt. What can we do as women to elevate self-doubt? A very familiar scripture is the life of Esther. She was a powerful woman who knew she had to do what she had to do.

She knew that what she was about to do was against protocol, but she did it and saved her people. What if Esther said, "No, I can't do this. I don't have the power within." I know she had some fear. But she did not let her fear overcome the plan. This is what she did. She went and gathered together all the Jews that were present in Shushan, and "fast ye for me, and neither eat nor drink three days, night or day: I also and my maidens will fast likewise; and so, will I go in unto the king, which is not according to the law: and if I perish, I perish" (Ester 4:16 King James Bible). She said, "If I perish, let me perish." We, too, as women, must get to the point where we are that confident with our lives. You see, Esther was not double-minded. Not one time did she doubt. She knew what she had to do, and she carried out the plan. We should let nothing, or anyone stop us from pursing our dreams. Here a few steps to help you get rid of self-doubt:

A. Present your body as a living sacrifice that is holy and acceptable to God.

B. Do not be conformed to this world.

C. Be transformed by the renewing of your mind.

I truly believe, as women of God, we must follow the pattern. We must be the example the world needs to see. We must understand our service is unto God. The total person is living for God. Once we make up our minds that we are living for God, there is no room for self-doubt. Your creator has designed you to be a designer original. There is no one else like you. You have a purpose; you have a plan. The blueprint is already laid out. I want you to know that, if you are looking for love, it is in you. You must realize that. You must know that. When everyone else is gone and you are alone, you will just have you. You must deal with you. You must want to deal with you. You must know that God is always with you. He loves you unconditionally. You must love yourself like never before.

As we are closing our twenty-one-day journey to "Looking for Love in all the Right Place" know that, if any of you lack wisdom, let him ask of God, who gives to all liberally and without reproach, and it will be given to him. But let him ask in faith, with no doubting, for he who doubts is like a wave of the sea driven and tossed by the wind. For let not that man suppose that he will receive anything from the Lord; he is a double-minded man, unstable in all his ways" (James 1:5 World English Bible).

**Affirmation:**

I am not double-minded.

I am confident.

I am in love with me.

I am in love with God.

**Prayer:** For God so loved (put your name there) the world that He gave His only begotten son that whosoever (put your name there) Believeth in Him should not perish but will have everlasting life. Lord, thank You for giving me beauty for ashes. Lord, I thank You for loving me unconditionally. I thank You for being my Abba Father, My Lord, My Lover, and My Friend. Amen.

Made in the USA
Middletown, DE
19 March 2024